Reading Poets

Vic Pickup is the author of *Lost & Found* (Hedgehog Press, 2020), *What Colour is My Brain?* (Hedgehog Press 2022) and *The Omniscient Tooth Fairy* (Indigo Dreams, 2023). She is co-organiser of Poets Café Reading and the town's Stanza group.

@vicpickup
www.vicpickup.com

Reading Poets

A New Anthology

Edited by Vic Pickup

Also by Two Rivers Poets

David Attwooll, *The Sound Ladder* (2015)
Charles Baudelaire, *Paris Scenes* translated by Ian Brinton (2021)
William Bedford, *The Dancers of Colbek* (2020)
Kate Behrens, *Man with Bombe Alaska* (2016)
Kate Behrens, *Penumbra* (2019)
Kate Behrens, *Transitional Spaces* (2022)
Conor Carville, *English Martyrs* (2019)
David Cooke, *A Murmuration* (2015)
David Cooke, *Sicilian Elephants* (2021)
Tim Dooley, *Discoveries* (2022)
Jane Draycott, *Tideway* (re-issued 2022)
Jane Draycott & Lesley Saunders, *Christina the Astonishing* (re-issued 2022)
Claire Dyer, *The Adjustments* (2024)
Claire Dyer, *Yield* (2021)
John Froy, *The Blue Armchair* (2024)
John Froy, *Sandpaper & Seahorses* (2018)
James Harpur, *The Examined Life* (2021)
Maria Teresa Horta, *Point of Honour* translated by Lesley Saunders (2019)
Ian House, *Just a Moment* (2020)
Philippe Jaccottet, *In Winter Light* translated by Tim Dooley (2022)
Rosie Jackson, *Love Leans over the Table* (2023)
Rosie Jackson & Graham Burchell, *Two Girls and a Beehive: Poems about Stanley Spencer and Hilda Carline* (2020)
Martha Kapos, *Music, Awake Her* (2024)
Gill Learner, *Chill Factor* (2016)
Gill Learner, *Change* (2021)
Sue Leigh, *Chosen Hill* (2018)
Sue Leigh, *Her Orchards* (2021)
Becci Louise, *Octopus Medicine* (2017)
Mairi MacInnes, *Amazing Memories of Childhood, etc.* (2016)
Steven Matthews, *On Magnetism* (2017)
Steven Matthews, *Some Other Where* (2023)
Henri Michaux, *Storms under the Skin* translated by Jane Draycott (2017)
Kate Noakes, *Goldhawk Road* (2023)
René Noyau, *Earth on Fire and other Poems* translated by Gérard Noyau with Peter Pegnall (2021)

James Peake, *Reaction Time of Glass* (2019)
James Peake, *The Star in the Branches* (2022)
David Ricks, *With Signs Following* (2024)
Peter Robinson & David Inshaw, *Bonjour Mr Inshaw* (2020)
Peter Robinson, *English Nettles* (re-issued 2022)
Peter Robinson, *Retrieved Attachments* (2023)
Lesley Saunders, *Nominy-Dominy* (2018)
Lesley Saunders, *This Thing of Blood & Love* (2022)
Jack Thacker, *Handling* (2018)
Robin Thomas, *The Weather on the Moon* (2022)
Susan Utting, *The Colour of Rain* (2024)
Jean Watkins, *Precarious Lives* (2018)

First published in the UK in 2024 by Two Rivers Press
7 Denmark Road, Reading RG1 5PA.
www.tworiverspress.com

This selection and Introduction © Vic Pickup 2024
Copyright for individual poems belongs to the author of the poem.

The rights of the individual poets to be identified as the authors of their works have been asserted by them in accordance with the Copyright, Designs and Patents Act of 1988.

All rights reserved. No part of this publication may be reproduced, stored in or introduced into a retrieval system, or transmitted, in any form, or by any means (electronic, mechanical, photocopying, recording or otherwise) without the prior written permission of the publisher.

ISBN 978-1-915048-13-4

1 2 3 4 5 6 7 8 9

Two Rivers Press is represented in the UK by Inpress Ltd and distributed by BookSource, Glasgow.

Cover image: 'Ruin Abbey 4' (2019) by Michael Garaway, watercolour and acrylic, 85mm × 120mm

Cover design by Nadja Robinson
Text design by Nadja Robinson and typeset in Janson and Parisine

Printed and bound in Great Britain by TJ Books, Padstow

Acknowledgements

There are a great many people I wish to thank for their part in the creation of this anthology.

First and foremost, I would like to express my gratitude to all those who sent poetry during the open submission window. The process of selection was much more challenging than I had expected, with consideration being paid for the symbiosis between poems as well as their individual merit. Many poems I enjoyed did not make it through the many 'rounds' of conference between myself and the panel; there were some wonderful works which simply could not be squeezed in, but without those submissions we would not have had such a feast from which to taste.

My thanks to author and poet Claire Dyer who helped with the selection and editing process, giving her time and wisdom generously.

To the Two Rivers team, namely Anne Nolan as chief hand-holder, alongside Peter Robinson, Sally Castle and Nadja Robinson for their guidance and expertise in the production of the creation you hold in your hands. I think we can agree the result is indeed a thing of beauty.

And to artist Michael Garaway, whose depiction of the Reading abbey ruins and town's skyline crowns the finished work most beautifully. Do visit his website at www.garaway.co.uk to see more.

Thank you also to Barbara Morris for her kind hospitality and strong coffee (always needed!).

And, lastly – to you, Reader, for picking up a copy of *Reading Poets*. We hope you enjoy the treasures within.

Contents

Introduction by Vic Pickup | xiii

Liam Anslow-Sucevic
  Passenger | 2
  The Beginning of This Century | 3

Kate Behrens
  The Invisible Girl | 4
  Memory Machinery | 5

Denise Bundred
  Le Café de Nuit | 6
  After the Crows | 7

J. A. Clothier
  A New Town | 8
  Sonnet for a Drag Queen | 10

Maisie Crittenden
  monkey's paw | 11
  stable hand | 12

Marcin Czyż
  Oxford Rd | 13
  Goodnight in Lublin | 14

Fiona Dignan
  40.2 | 15
  Preserving | 16

Jo Farrant
  Quantum physics, or something | 17
  Light Touch | 18

John Froy
  Deep Ecology | 20
  Dawn Chorus | 21

Anastasia Gale
  Cases for Shapeshifters | 22
  Venus | 23

Martin Haslam
  El Castillo | 24
  Yugen | 25

Kitty Hawkins
  Snippets of Eve | 26
  To Live | 27

Megan Hay
  Pressure | 28
  Hallway Fantasies | 29

Frances Hudson
  Burnt Rice | 30
  A Broken Appointment Explained | 31

Karen Izod
  Dark Skies Reserve | 32
  It must have been August | 33

Andrew Jamison
  To Lime Pickle | 34
  Badminton Water Fight in the Garden, January | 35

Charlotte Johnson
  Let's Go, Rockets | 36
  Tea-towel | 38

Zannah Kearns
  Home | 39
  Song for Marina | 40

Gill Learner
  December | 41
  Night crime | 42

Katherine Meehan
   Working Together We Can Achieve Anything! | 43
   A Rumination with a View | 44

Kate Noakes
   Self-portrait in *Lawrence of Arabia* | 46
   Self-portrait in the Union bar | 47

Louise Ordish
   Seven friends and what they talked about | 48
   It comes up at the end of the session | 49

Patrick Osada
   Snapshots | 50
   When shadowed days are done | 52

Lillie Postlewhite
   'When orange is the sky' | 53
   Inevitable | 54

Victoria Pugh
   A pub in Wales | 55
   The enemy within | 57

Kate Pursglove
   Curlews | 58
   Stanley's War | 59

Susan Roberts
   The Wrong Way Round | 60
   The Ides of March | 61

Lesley Saunders
   Putting You in the Picture | 62
   The Other Woman | 63

Geoff Sawers
   Wounded Sky | 64
   Ton Up No Lights | 65

Isobel Shirlaw
  When Christ Came to Glastonbury | 66
  Candle | 67

Megan Slater
  the something unsaid | 68
  the night-walk exhibition | 69

Antonia Taylor
  Emily in Paris, too | 71
  Spring lunchtimes, I knew you'd be waiting | 72

Robin Thomas
  Absolutely Everything | 74
  Gedicht gefunden | 75

Susan Utting
  The Colour of Dark | 76
  Wired for Sound | 77

Jean Watkins
  Llanrhaeadr | 78
  Tulips | 79

Ann Westgarth
  Cor Cordium (Heart of Hearts) | 80
  How to hang Ruth Ellis | 82

Jules Whiting
  The Gift of Darkness | 83
  Rather than video games | 84

Contributors | 86

Introduction

'The power of art is that it can connect us to one another, and to larger truths about what it means to be alive and what it means to be human.'
— Daniel Levitin

You have in your hands a book written by thirty-seven people of different ages, from a broad range of backgrounds, and who draw upon a rich tapestry of unique experiences in the creation of their work. These poets are united here, not only by a shared connection with Reading, but also by the desire to use words to touch their reader and forge a sense of belonging through that recognition.

The formation of this anthology was no easy task; Reading's arts scene is alive and buzzing, and the submissions were abundant. Come along to any of the many poetry events which take place in our town and you'll bear witness to the inclusive and welcoming environment that has been nurtured by passionate volunteers over the years. These opportunities to share have facilitated a thriving community of wordsmiths and poetry-lovers.

Two Rivers Press wanted to harness this energy and celebrate the diversity of Reading's poetry scene by curating a body of work which represents just some of the writers who have lived, are still living or merely passing through our town at the time of its creation.

It's a happy accident that the title of this collection has two interpretations: you needn't be local to enjoy reading what's written here – reading poets is for anyone, anywhere. The poems in this book serve to unite us, putting all demographics aside to connect on a human level, observing the insignificant details of the everyday, pondering the bigger questions, presenting the ability to see and be seen.

Contributors within these pages hail from Ireland, America, South Africa and Poland. We have among them a retired cardiologist, stage technician and journalist, as well as carers, students and artists. Some of the poets have been published many times, and they stand beside others for whom this will be their first time in print. Our youngest writer is eighteen, our oldest in their eighties. Each of these individuals has crafted and selected two poems, enabling them to give a little of who they are to you, the reader, in the hope that you will find something to love, to evoke thought, to take with you.

The cover art by Michael Garaway complements the sentiment behind this collection beautifully. Through the depiction of our everyday urban scenes using the careful composition of colour and texture, Michael's paintings provide 'a much-needed presentation of stillness, contemplation and ordered calm'. The image on the front of this book gives a taste for the many distilled moments and thoughts captured within it from a myriad of voices.

I'm truly proud of what has been created in *Reading Poets: A New Anthology*. This book exists as a testimony to the vibrant and welcoming arts scene in Reading, as well as a celebration for all those making so much happen in our wonderful town.

Vic Pickup

Reading Poets

Passenger

Beyond this train's faintly finger-printed window, a blur of stones
    jut from a hillside in umber, slate-grey, black.

This seven-second stretch of cemetery has at its centre a yellow
    digger; it empties the earth to store more of our dead.

Suddenly, I catch sight of the light as it pulses across a green field,
    while at the same time my mind turns towards those stones.

Liam Anslow-Sucevic

The Beginning of This Century

A cool light pours through the blinds
on a leather chair, where a woman rests
in the indents of her late husband's form.

The dimmed television exhibits another war.
A camera pans around bodies as pixels,
ballistic missiles jet through the air.

Her mind flickers with pictures
of the bombings she witnessed:
factories riven, singed-ochre glow.

The aroma of slow-roasted lamb
twists through her nose and throat,
drifting to the stench of metal.

Liam Anslow-Sucevic

The Invisible Girl

Their design was alive, it wore her in,
so she became
invisible: colour and material
exchanged for a vanishing.

She was the long grey skirt
(italicised shadow
stumbling along the streets to school),
or shit-brown of knitted buttons,
ludic flowers above a fringed hem;

she swapped her skin
for cable stitches, unreflecting
red of velvet, the perfect pitch
of cords' 'sea-green.'

And when she was crêpe-de-chine,
or breast bone of fake silk,
she slid
towards a flickering power,

where two of them gave credence
to someone that really lived
inside this stuff, for minutes, or hours.

Kate Behrens

Memory Machinery

You hover between white spaces,
remember assemblages
that joined, forever, some refrain
to a dress or address,
some hope to the look of the hidden,
glinting.

Today, in the snowy road,
a partridge sits as if on an egg,
refusing to move as my car
slows –
it takes time to realise

the wings are broken, have frozen it
into a child's idea
of bird, but amid bewildered friends,
its head held high
(as if embarrassed by death),

all of this pinned to a certain light
in mid-December, a kink
in the future road.

Kate Behrens

Le Café de Nuit

'I've tried to express the idea that the café is a place where you can
ruin yourself, go mad, commit crimes.'
— Vincent to Theo van Gogh, September 1888

Night-prowlers drink absinthe under furious orange gaslight.
The clock is set at quarter past twelve. This room is alive

to the palette of dark hours, despair in abandoned glasses. He imbibes
Japanese prints with his wine; relishes their empty spaces, thick outlines

and instinctive contrasts so he clears the floor, fills the boards
with yellow impasto, creates discordant reds – from blood

to pink – which clash with disparate greens to heighten self-doubt.
This is not a place for rest. Terrible passions resound.

Why should he give others ease? Anxiety bleeds into each tilted surface.
'An ugly picture', he confides to his brother who takes him at his word.

Vincent calculates just how much disquiet to pour into bottles at the bar,
pushed-back chairs, the jaundiced-white jacket of M. Ginoux who guards

the carambole table and its shadow, and knows time will crawl
until he can snatch ten minutes on the couch behind the curtain

before he must serve breakfast to the postman, reapers, quarry miners
and other citizens who have something going right in their lives.

Denise Bundred

'Le Café de Nuit' by Vincent van Gogh (1888)
https://artgallery.yale.edu/collections/objects/12507

After the Crows

He sets the easel between cone-shaped sheaves
rests his rucksack on the stubbled earth and stands
shoulder to shoulder with shocks of wheat.

>   A wealth of canvases so he joins two
>   paints a panorama of the field again
>   within a week of the storm-flung crows.

He inhales fresh-cut corn and rubs a grain
between finger and thumb before releasing it
paint-stained, into sandy soil.

>   Indifferent to the piercing stalks underfoot
>   he mixes gentle violet for the long shadows
>   and citron for the flood of golden light.

He is of the scene, working like a reaper in a straw hat.
Instead of scythe and twine, his tool is a palette knife
and he transcribes his lifeless companions into oil.

>   United in mortality, yet they endure.
>   The catalogue number suggests this is the final scene
>   although no letters remain from these last days.

We only know that Vincent sees the harvest in –
before he picks up the gun.

Denise Bundred

'Sheaves of Wheat' by Vincent van Gogh (1890)
https://vangoghgallery.com/catalog/Painting/487/Sheaves-of-Wheat.html

A New Town

I moved to a new town, just me and mum
And documented every one
From Red and Blue to Moon and Sun
I didn't know what I'd begun

So many small hours spent in the Belle de Nuit
Hat-down holidays in occupied Paris
Guns and gangs in pastille Miami
Heists in Prague, Shanghai, and Delhi,

Over the German trenches I flew
For a couple of months in '42
Starting eleven in '66
Making history is how I get my kicks

I toppled monarchies in far-off galaxies
Built up empires from principalities
Saved the world from untold fatalities
In a million hand-made, mad realities

U-boats in the Amazon,
A gun fight through the Louvre
A spinning shell shoots past
My five-point drift manoeuvre

I can dive, I can fly, defend or attack,
I'm a small, knitted man made of buttons and sack,
I'm everything, everywhere, turning logic in knots,
My journey guided by old Alan Watts

There's intrigue, heartbreak, betrayal, and glee,
There's war and there's peace and there's trade and there's tea,
I can pause it all to go for a wee,
Me and my old trusty Playstation 3

The couch is a space ship, a war zone, a mind
I'm anywhere else, but I'm comfy, reclined,
Mysteries and sport, interplanetary beings,
Folded in half and tucked in my jeans

Snowboarding mountains, endless, alone,
All from wherever I've carried my phone
It's private, it's social, it often courts looks,
But it's better than telly and movies and books,

And music and dancing and stories and riddles,
Cause it's all those together with me in the middle

They think I wither and shrink when I play
But I move to a new town every day

J.A. Clothier

Sonnet for a Drag Queen

The glossy raspberry pink bag stares at me
Well-worn, by its contents only standing

Narcissian pool hung flat against the screen
Solar ring round the mirror blinding

Unfurl the brushes, bring the palettes out
The pencils and the powder and the gold

Contours carved in colour, painted on pout
The geometry of being, written bold

Mixing the light and the dark on my face
Caravaggio contrasting the shades

Your countenance, mandala in its place
A sculpture worked with gel and paint and blades

Now she is who you are and proudly worn
A stain around the sink come Sunday morn

J. A. Clothier

monkey's paw

i am my father's son
cursed to be my mother's daughter
these hands should not be mine
someone else should
possess them

treat them carefully
moisturise the once soft skin
ornate the ends to a point of principle
putting them past the practical

i should be
draped in oversized clothing
swinging a sword at the armies
hidden behind the bench at the back of our garden
i should be digging out the trenches
instead of planting the roses

i lean on tiptoes over the kitchen counter
all my insignificant weight on small elbows
i jump and scamper
careful not to scratch the plastic cupboard coverings
ambling my way to the window

here still i sit still
watching him drink at the end of the bar
while i discuss Aldi opening times and Primark sales
he pretends to understand the football
i've been playing for ten years

his friends all have sons
he has me

somehow that is worse

Maisie Crittenden

stable hand

all the tears my father's never shed
left to boil in a
                limestone-rotted kettle
salty bitterness
lemon and tequila
                  he doesn't quite get the joke

doesn't swing his fists
or dance to Joy Division
                    a white golf ball flies off
he meanders on behind it

humming songs about stableboys serenading a
                half price horse that he'll never ride
the cheapest apples off the market
                    rotting against an extravagant coat

silent rage
electric toaster
no lips, tongue, or teeth
                left on the marble counter

the house is quiet
              shoelaces remain untied
the milk never finds a way to the bowl
          that old cow
                never does come home

Maisie Crittenden

Oxford Rd

In memoriam Józef Czyż (1937–2023)

Oxford Road the horizontal arm of the Union Jack
what isn't there?
there are doctors from Poland at number 603
including a venereologist specialised in the tropical
and the Caribbean syph
ten numbers further under 613 blaze the feverish wombs of Club 613's
permanent residents sisters of mercy
I met a girl from Barbados
thanks to a super expensive English teacher
I effected a booze coup exchanging Captain Grant
for Mont Gay est. 1703 Barbados Rum which makes lips taste better
producing English words with a Caribbean accent.

Marcin Czyż

Translated from Polish to English by Antywanda from Rotterdam

Goodnight in Lublin

In memoriam Józef Czechowicz*

The tea is getting cold but the time is not
time is drinking up yet another cup of tea

the evening will end
in a dark surface before your eyes
where they say one has the best rest

no tea is drunk
sometimes only a poem is being read at bedtime
the one with the city's solitude in the poet's meadow

sleeping time is drinking
more softly.

Marcin Czyż

Translated from Polish to English by Andrij Saveneć

* Józef Czechowicz (1903–1939) was a Polish avant-garde poet. His poetry is an extraordinary mix between an arcadian and apocalyptic, with uniqe sounds of the melody of the Polish language.

40.2

This summer Death came by degrees
creeping up through the same digits
children chant from blackboards like benedictions
reconfigured into tarmac running like oil
and the seedlings we planted shrivelled
to accusations. I promise
we can plant new ones
as though fecundity is a party trick
we minor gods play with a sleight of hand.
Even though the seabirds and the whales and
the indigenous peoples have been
the canaries in the coal mine for decades. Even now
the corals are apparitions, we can go tell the bees
it's a record-breaking summer. And we play
with platitudes and pretend drinking soya milk in our lattes
washes our hands of guilt, whilst playing Icarus with our short haul
flights to the sun. I buy the kids fans and coat them
in SPF as some kind of contrition, whilst they draw smiling suns
that give us papercuts.
We wear our language lightly and say
It'll be snowing next week and, *Back in '76*, but
the blackberries have come early like bruises and stain
our fingers as the leaves turn in late July. Now I wash
the milk cartons more carefully and fold my cardboard
with something like reverence before placing it as an offering
to the green recycling bin
as though confessing my sins.

Fiona Dignan

Preserving

Late August comes in abundance, mellows
the light, even our language drips
from thick tongues, clotted words ripe
with sugar – *tomorrow, tomorrow*
plenty, there's plenty of time.
Everything swollen and heavy. Earthed
hands work the land, stripping back
wheat to stubble, bales like cotton reels stitching
the last of summer to the soil. Clods
of sheep litter the hills, leaking
bleats into the blue –
soon, soon – their languid cream
can't last, their coats will soon grow
bleak with mud. All that plumpness
will split and spool. The wasps come
with their petty tensions and the nights
imperceptibly close in, their sudden chill
tightening the air at dusk. The urge creeps in
to preserve, enclose – seal
the softness in; bronzed limbs salted
in the last sea swim, canning
the berries and beans, retreating, retreating.
Spiders begin to weave, webs vibrating with
small deaths. *Not long now* –
the brittle branches will bear
the lightness of empty nests. Still –

in the mortuary white of the winter months, the bud
and root and lamb lie enclosed.
The potential of new abundance preserved
within the ending.

Fiona Dignan

Quantum physics, or something

Energy absorbed by *you matter* to this
molecular parent made up of the same
stuff as Angel Delight. The pressure

between two points and their centre
where adventure happens (meaning legs)
pressed up on the couch with silted tea.

A child takes calls in their room to not
disturb the pressure, sandpaper saves
the creases for later. Energy absorbed

by your mattering to Mum's collection
of scarves (meaning lost legs), the search
for a third place like hers. The pressure

to road trip down tinted palm lines and find
the scene where you always cry, when
the child falls asleep inside/ inside/ inside.

Jo Farrant

Light Touch

It's like this, it's like clacking teeth,
on a warm journey, plugging pens
from my pocket into train station sockets
with a straw stuck down a stranger's mouth.

It's juggling a lover's bones inside
their hands like a circus act. My cheek
on your arm like a hoover on carpet,
unclean and nice. It's not quite that
it's more like here,

on a deck chair in the breathy dark
with the Twilight soundtrack on
for the hundredth time.

It's a dozen light bulbs
stacked in
a carton of eggs,
breakfast with
the mouse your cat left
at the doorstep.
It's going to museums
wanting to touch, like
the plants growing fast
around listed buildings.
It's nearing the end of
your favourite series
knowing you'll have to
say goodbye.

When you sat on the floor the last time
you heard TV static and wrapped
VHS tape around your fingers
like a fruit Winder, it's that first fight
with your imaginary friend,
it's kind of like this, like if you spoke
too quick with a burnt tongue
and if you never said goodbye.

Jo Farrant

Deep Ecology

We walked across the ancient land, talking
of Gaia, our earth mother, in uncertain April

and of his family perishing in Warsaw,
his old dad who got out ... It began to snow.

Each snowflake is alive, you know, loaded with bacteria
returning from the upper air.

And we came to the village of Melbury Bubb,
a clock-stopped church tower under the hill,

looked for signs of green men on the Celtic font,
in a disused chalk pit found sea creatures far older;

a plant world in miniature clings to the cliff there
only growing as big as it dares, as fits its niche.

Snow swirling, we climbed the wood-crowned Bubb;
deer leapt away; we picked wild ramsons, just enough.

That's when he said, glancing to the east
he would've lived back then. Before the Common Era.

When humans born small remained so,
when little was enough for us all.

I saw a giant, barefoot, spreadeagled on the ground.

John Froy

Dawn Chorus

Listen Ma, I'm in the buttoned armchair,
the green velvet one that he upholstered,
with his letters about you spread on my knee.

We've had tea, been up to town,
seen the best church in Devon.

I was out on the Common, 4.30 a.m.
as I aim to be once each spring,
this time, in time.

I was there when they began,
down where the path turns and dips –
that equinoctial tide of birdsong.

In a hawthorn, two young thrushes
practised their simple repetitions.
There were garden warblers, blackcaps.

You must be there at the beginning,
when the first one calls and the echo comes,
another and another.

Sing with me now.

John Froy

Cases for Shapeshifters

It is only under street lamps
where we become chameleons.

The red dog shifts to shades of blue,
a land creature born from the sea
and left to roam beneath the light
with but a single wise-working eye.

The wandering mind that lapses
and stumbles into technicolour,
the story of a visionary
crafted by a streak in the dark.

The automaton turned human,
clipping copper against concrete
a broken vocal box – a larynx –
repeating notes about sunshine.

The 'we' becoming 'us'
that trudges toward the solitary 'I'
the poet, the linguist, the lonely one
without a word in the night.

Anastasia Gale

Venus

This high up
she could see that they were wrong.

The moon never meets the ocean.
There is never a moment where that lonely white ball
is awarded the pleasure
of such a meeting in confidence.
If not there, then where does the sea end?
She had thought that it stretched out
grasping at the wisps of the sky
just enough to tickle a wave.
But now, she was unsure;
What if it tried and tipped off the edge,
tired, all too hopeful for tenderness
and stuck to the sand?
What if it forgot that it is violent,
unpredictable and all too angry
to try and grab that stuck flag?
What if it got scared of it cracking
flexing a watery wrist before the rounded eggshell,
that damned bright glass dome, the guide of all tides.
Most of all, she felt sorry for the myths
she had been told. The lying love stories
of how the Moon and Sea met after the fourth day
and had spent their nights tangled together ever since.

She felt most sorry for Venus,
who stood on that shell
and breezed through her existence
thinking that it was a testament of glory.
But it was not. It was a relic of trying.

Anastasia Gale

El Castillo

Our phones and knowingness won't help us
in the gravid darkness of the cave.

Here are bison, horses, deer and auroch, ibex,
hands! Hands splayed. Hands on the rock,

like ours that hold our wavering lights,
and fresh as dawn and ancient.

What are we seeing? Fetishes or eidolons,
perhaps a sympathetic hex that's human

and beyond our grasp.
                              Lit by marrow flame
those hands that rubbed red haematite

and charcoal scrapes on candid walls
were instinct with a touch, a vision

that our fumbling tip-tap fingers
can't recall, can't know. These images

are phantom gestures, eloquent, ancestral,
rocky mute. Just that they are is plenty.

Martin Haslam

Yugen

Something about the rain today –
the smear of light and memory –

brings back the golden bracken and a shift
of mist hung on the bulk of Pavey Ark,

its rocky furrows charmed in sinking sun;
and the two of us elated, aching, young,

who'd watched the creep of shadow on the crag
wipe out the lines we'd grappled up till darkness

falling, down we'd come. More than the thrill
of scrambling up that face was on us

in those moments as we watched the dusk
unspell our intimate redoubt. And now

my purchase is in books I find a word
that's just.
               For what we may have felt.
For what we almost knew.

Martin Haslam

Yugen: a term from Japanese aesthetics expressing
an almost ineffable concept, something like:
'a profound mysterious sense of the beauty of the universe …
and the sad beauty of human suffering'.

Snippets of Eve

After Michelangelo's The Creation of Adam

At the gallery the dude deems the old guy *pretty gangster*,
suggests to his friend-zoned arm-candy,
we should get one done of you. *Mate*.

Kitchen. Hub of the housewarming.
Existential pockets where we'd best not go.
Thin-scarfed art boys gloat about the pulling power of Greek.

One specimen educates me on sonnets. *How they rhyme.*
I worry if I don't have a daughter I'll lose my grip on Mum.

*

Corinne deals with broken glass on the back doormat,
avoids the dew pellets on the lawn that mock her –

Shards of women who raised us fill our conversation:
auburn-haired furies manning an orange Beetle,
sirens
– runaways.

South Tottenham's sun malnourished and choking
on an adolescent Saturday night, Corinne says,
sifting pebbles, *I wonder why my mother doesn't like me.*

I repeat a biting prophecy whispered at each daughter's birth:
No one loves their mother till she dies.

Kitty Hawkins

To Live

When our first school closed down
two double writing desks, two chairs,
and a square wooden table came home.
Paint spills hold residual memories:
Sunday afternoon Warhammer,
Mum, two sons, a daughter, equal on all sides.

One writing desk is the keeper of keys
torso lifting to reveal phone book,
address scraps, dust, names
discarded and forgotten.
Most are in Mum's script –
legible without trying.

Strange places mosaiced
on Wright's DIY or JP & Sons'
A5 sun-bleached rule.
Strange places she's been.
A life remembered in postcodes
and further on from that –

'Moon River' on her father's deathbed,
the melody a palimpsest
cloaking the words she needed to speak
but couldn't say.

Kitty Hawkins

Pressure

Between thumb, finger,
and an absent mind,
I crush tender sloe berries
and walk until time solidifies.

Their purple skins burst like split lips,
staining palms and worries with a
gratification so wet, and so mauve,
that my flesh itches for more.

In this stagnant place I wonder
how much longer I have left,
'til some other wanderer decides
that I too must be compressed.

Megan Hay

Hallway Fantasies

I want the hallway
to fill with thick smoke
when I re-emerge at last,

to draw the glittering
strangers off the street,
so they can find me

with the paintings,
puckered at the edges
like dried plasters,

pasted on to be
passed around in
high-pitch conversation,

frantically gratified
in the glass of
judgement-drunk eyes,

inescapable mirror balls:
they can't look away
and neither can I.

An exhibition of
dry-eyed stalemate,
a life for a life,

an addict in an art gallery,
searching for answers
in the whites of blurry eyes.

Megan Hay

Burnt Rice

The rice burned in the microwave as she stood at the mirror,
painstakingly daubing paste the same colour as the canvas on the canvas.
In the microwave the rice burned, whilst all she knew is she wished
   she was thinner,
tossing and turning like mice nestled in the craters of their Swiss-cheese
   homes asleep.
Burning rice and microwaves and the belief that 'to be pretty is to be
   a winner',
and wielding lipstick like lavender swaying in polluted air or ballet dancing
   in thick smog.
All the while the rice is burnt and the microwave's on fire and there's
   nothing left for dinner.
Such a sorry waste, pellets charred until crisp and hard, rubbery,
   soil-coloured and smoking.
Such a pretty face painted so pleasantly and precise, glowing, rosy
   and nice at the mirror
as the rice burned in the microwave.

Frances Hudson

A Broken Appointment Explained

A response to 'A Broken Appointment' by Thomas Hardy

                    I was simply running late,
time swooping by in one curved eight, making me miss our date.
In no way was it intentional, malicious, planned, meant to anger you;
when the track of the ticking clock was a thing I forgot to suppose –
it was an accident please believe, let my deepest apologies ensue –
I didn't guess you'd come to this conclusion. Dear, heaven only knows
all things small and insignificant, plus the truth which looms so great:
                    I was simply running late.

                    I was on the way,
and my phone was dead – of course – and so I could not say
to wait, to not misconstrue this as deliberate. I could not warn
you of my late arrival which broke your heart and ruined your day.
It was a surprise that for you such deep suspicion was so quickly born,
love torn instantly – a mistake for which you cut me off straight away,
                    (Alas, I'm sorry! Yet now at least you know…)
                    I was on the way!

Frances Hudson

Dark Skies Reserve

I can't quite say what it is I am looking for,
my eye is too naked, too untrained
to fathom these distances.
I wish I were more knowing.

Time is a greedy forager; it gathers more
than it needs in the sable softness
of this night sky. Darkness pushes
at my face, closes in

where a hammock moon lies on its back,
strung low across the cow sheds, rising to await
its nightly milking by lovers and poets,

and dodging the debris, forever hurtling through skies
where there is no sleep to clean up its cosmic act
nor reward its luminosity.

An echo of owls is claiming the fields
as our ghostly band of stars reaches through
and there is Jupiter, the reliable one.

Karen Izod

It must have been August

The laundry was piling up; no one could bear
to sleep in the same linen twice, as if we carried
the soiling on our bodies.

Later, I strung up the line in the orchard, pegged out
the sheets in the way she did, letting them billow
in the high summer breeze.

In the freezer I found her neatly labelled tubs:
gooseberries, rhubarb, such small amounts.
I took the children out to the fields;

we were adventurers, swishing the long grass
with our swords, valiant, until we saw the snake
curled up in the heat of the afternoon,

so still it could have been dead.
We turned back, it had unnerved us
too much.

Karen Izod

To Lime Pickle

Epitome of pizzazz, apotheosis
of citrus,

firecracker
poppadom ambassador,

you are
a tightrope walk between here and a star

of funky heat,
your flesh a punchy, hit-me beat

in a hit song
about what someone did all summer long

in a hot country
in their youth; you are a walk-in pantry,

lip smacker starter, beer washed down bounty;
if flavour was a state, or county.

Andrew Jamison

Badminton Water Fight in the Garden, January

And who says you can't play badminton
in the garden with your son in January
if he wants although he's only three
and can't hit the shuttlecock and doesn't know the rules
or enough numbers to keep score,
would rather stamp on the net, stamp on it
and beat the racket into the soft ground
shouting, 'TENNIS!' before dragging it along
the patio slabs despite your protestations,
calling for the water pistols, the blue one,
and the red one, and to fill it, and to fill it
until it bubbles up over the top, gushes
ice-cold over your hand and trousers and shoe.
There was a time this would have bothered you.

Andrew Jamison

Let's Go, Rockets

Here's to being just too tired for this thanks to a Friday night resolve
    to party hard, to smearing
on make up in the rear-view mirror because the other mums always
    look nice

Here's to wearing coats inside because sports halls are only warm
    if you are in shorts and a vest
to swearing at the stupid sat-nav lady and clocking up all those
    extra miles

Here's to delayed tip-offs because referees don't ever account for traffic
    or limited parking
to the pounding pounding on the court, in perfect time with last night's
    wine

Here's to no noise being louder than a ball bouncing bouncing bouncing
    on a wooden floor
and to coaches yelling about where there is and isn't the space that
    no player ever finds

Here's to shouting shouting, *Find your man* and *Box out* and *33*
    whatever that is
and laughing with your husband about there never being a 69

Here's to pheromones and frustration, hormones and all that blaming
thundering up and down, up and down, and hanging out at the
    free-throw line

Here's to strategically placing yourself away from the overly-chatty
    dad, only
to over-chat at some other dad who was just looking for a bit
    of phone time

Here's to rebounds rebounds, nothing but net and FOUL – *surely, Ref*
and to, *Let's Go Rockets, Let's Go* ... for the 99th time

Here's to fantasy murder of opposition mums cheering on their sons
   so proud
and to stuffing 12 sweaty kits in the wash and to hanging them all in
   a line

Here's to that army of narrow-waisted shorts, skinny vests, uniform
   blood red.
Blood-filled vials relentlessly surrendered, month-on-month

Here's to probing and frustration, hormones and all that blaming
and, *You're not young anymore, you know*

Here's to cutting alcohol completely and to strictly scheduled intercourse
pound pound, negative test result month-on-month and finally

Here's to catching one lucky break
chanting chanting, *Let's Go Rockets, Let's Go* ...

Charlotte Johnson

Tea-towel

Crumbed, crumpled robins, some in linen flight
some sporting soup stains or beetroot scars, ripped
where one met a newly sharpened knife, red
breasts, heaped onto themselves.
Too jaded to be Christmas.

Charlotte Johnson

Home

There is a way a house seems to settle
    after the last guest is gone.
A quietude of relief, for some – a calm
    floating down like the parachutes
of a dandelion, or a scattering
    of white blossoms at the far end of the garden
where lawn slopes into stream.

She wonders if it will ever be that way for her,
    the emptiness a balm, a kind of yielding.
Each day she feels his loss all over again –
    too tired to keep pretending he's just left the room,
about to return with tea for two on a tray,
    a second slice of madeira.

How he'd loved entering rooms filled with people,
    the man she lived more with than without.
Now, the funeral's done, the buffet gone, and everyone
    is waved off with families of their own.
Soon the phone will ring in the hall – the children,
    calling to say they're home.

Zannah Kearns

Song for Marina

That it's come to this, Marina, protector
of daughters, heartsore and weary;
the lengths to which love must journey.

We wait for you here as you tear your heart
into strips, dismantle your life
with one last kiss, one last embrace.

Which piece of him do you carry, he who now
beds down in a bunker, learns to take aim?
What of you is left in his keeping?

Sheets, fresh and white, billow then fall
across these beds. We fill your rooms
with sunflowers, knowing it'll do nothing

to stop your grief pouring out through the open window
into the dark. But we'll build a summer for your girls,
plant this garden in them. When they look back,

years from now, they'll remember cowslips then lavender,
bees in the honeysuckle, jenny wrens and song thrushes,
the wooden swing hanging from the walnut tree.

Zannah Kearns

December

When the air is crisp as lettuce, wrap your scarf
more tightly, notice how grass is rimmed with frost
and faces blur in clouds of breath. At times
of drench and splash, try to be grateful for the rain
tap-dancing on your brolly or creeping down your neck:
it's feeding rivers, streams and lakes. When fog's fuzzying
the outlines of houses, churches, shops, view them
as impressionistic art. If the sun smiles, look up
into bare branches, see how twigs form lacy patterns,
black on white. On days when sleety winds brisk
from the east skittering burger-boxes down the street,
turn up your collar, remind yourself they rarely last.
And if it's grim to leave home before dawn, returning
after dark, give thanks for electricity and gas.
Through jackdaws' squawks and racketing,
listen for a blackbird's song at dusk as it arrives
earlier each day, a robin's lamplight melodies.
Once New Year partying is done, notice how
the days stretch out, little by little, towards spring.

Gill Learner

Night crime

He comes with cans of paint, thick marker pens,
a torch, stencils that jigsaw together to form images.
In this town he stretched a ladder high, traced
a black shape, filled detail in with white; he rolled on grey,
dabbed with a pen. A knotted sheet falls to a typewriter;
a man in broad-striped uniform slides towards
the dotted words that roll up from the paper feed.
Not Oscar, who served two years in a nearby cell
but an appeal for creative arts to occupy
the emptiness beyond.

The things the artist loves are walls – breeze-block,
limestone or red brick. But there's one he loathes:
the West Bank Barrier. Its concrete now flowers
with graffiti by him and artists from across the globe –
protesters smile from a muddle of slogans, cartoons,
pleas for peace, some skilled, some scrawled. Opposite,
in Bethlehem, he opened an hotel, called it the Walled Off.
He boasts it has the worst view in the world.

Gill Learner

Working Together We Can Achieve Anything!

Three of Pentacles

An artist, a monk, and a mason walk into a nave
and the artist breaks into a joke about Dorchester Abbey –
There was sex and booze and a prior who wouldn't behave…

Oh, the ladies kept coming and going through doors without keys!
The monk interrupts him, deadpan: *A toxic environment.*
And the mason laughs, and the artist swats at a bee.

The next day at work they show up with their blueprints
and diagrams. The weather is grey and they're bored;
sometimes they speak, more often they're silent.

Thinks the monk: *A cathedral's really no more than an airport –*
a liminal space with prayers instead of a plane
and the same long walk to the nearest toilet –

which is to say: we get closer to heaven
on a journey with people when our purpose is split
between lift off and descent.

And the mason's lungs put on their lining of dust
as he chisels his life's minutes into the archways.
This will take many lives; within a life, many lives can be lived.

The accretion of years and details turns stone into space,
thinks the artist, *but this is God's house; no one lives here.*
And he turns his ears to the endless drone of the bees.

Katherine Meehan

A Rumination with a View

Seven of Swords

'We have to endure the discordance between imagination
and fact. It is better to say, "I am suffering", than to say,
'This landscape is ugly".'
— Simone Weil

I spent a long time in a crowd of weapons.
Imagine my relief to be escorted
out of doors! To take up residence
on the mudflat, to live alone here,
to submit to this discomfort, determinedly,
to knot and re-knot my own restraints, so
I'll never be undone by the salt-wind
or cut my ties against two-sided people.

So, I don't know if it's safe to assume
the sea will not rise again in this direction;
it left some gungy tide pools to remind me
of its absent totality, how looking
inwards is the nature of the mind,
how every mind is separate, and this distance
makes me think of Harlech Castle – a holiday
someone took there years ago.

Okay, it wasn't a holiday.
It was a siege.
It's all in how you view it!
But if you stand still in one place
for long enough,
you can die of exhaustion,
like Edmund Mortimer
and most of his men.

In those days the waves came all the way
up to the castle. It took some centuries,
but the sea has since retreated, making space
for a golf course. Which begs the question:
if the sea can heave itself away from
the ramparts and form a different shoreline,
what's there to prevent my passage
through a door made out of swords?

Katherine Meehan

Self-portrait in *Lawrence of Arabia*

Unless you have the hand grasping
a pommel through the curtained saddle
of a camel, silver bracelets jangling,

or are one of the veiled women
ululating in full black on a rock side
in Wadi Rhum,

you are entirely absent –

even though another time you climbed
the red dunes, traced pictograms
scratched in those very cliffs

and watched a dung beetle trundle
through sand and stones at sunset.
Ah yes, the empty desert.

Kate Noakes

Self-portrait in the Union bar

This may've been before it was renamed,
The Nelson Mandela Bar, or at the gig
on its small stage by an up and coming Irish band,
who'd just released their first album.

You can't recall. But you do remember
the Boy in an ill-fitting jumble sale suit, ripped
t-shirt, suede ankle boots and dyed-black hair
who promised to love you.

And so he did for a very long time.
Until he said he didn't –

Perhaps his not buying you a pint
of snakebite that night was a clue.

Kate Noakes

Seven friends and what they talked about

There's the one who called us together. She says she's paused,
has days to herself, to listen to music, to shop,
has time on her hands, for now;
                                    and one who recalls
how she stood her ground, how she helped a man from prison;
and the man was seen, his torso bared, outside Tesco,
singing, *I'm free*;
                    and one who'll soon re-marry,
who'll use each ring of experience, of insight,
to keep this one safe;
                          and there's one who's swum so long
in the suffering of a marriage, spent her courage,
taken time, is taking the time it takes
to stay, to restart, to reinvent;
                          and there's one
whose family's a kaleidoscope that's turning.
A girl's a boy. The man's not as she thought.
And which coloured fragments are her?
                                and one is fusing
her old career with the new, finds both are a question
of how you get close to people, how close you get;

and there's one who came despite the just-lost girl.
She didn't, couldn't, speak of her, went early,
left us each a splash of her unbearable.

Louise Ordish

It comes up at the end of the session

My client talks of *jokey* and *going along with*.
I am listening – less with ears, more with body.
I sense *in-a-corner … powerless … small-and-scared*.
He continues with surface-talk, mild annoyance.
…and why, he says, *do I always think it's my fault?*
I choose to share what I've felt.
Everything slows.

I ask, *Do you know where that comes from?*
Everything stills.

His chin tips towards his chest and back.
A nod. A pause. Another. Five minutes left.

He breathes in through his nose and, slowly, out,
crosses his arms tightly against his body.
Both of us hunt for words, but which are the right ones?
We muddle, *I don't want to/You don't have to*,
crash of, *Never told anyone/Can if you want to*.
I try, *Also, we can talk about it*
without talking about it. Like we are now.

Louise Ordish

Snapshots

JULY

Driving the sticky surfaces of Summer,
with snapshot views of the Dashwood's hill;
curve and camber require attention,
glanced impressions of the parched brown fields.

Through the dusty screen July air shimmers:
distant copse turns blue mirage; here, beside
this sun scorched highroad, hedge-rowed willowherb
bows at my passing; magpies stroll the verge.

Undulating wheat with scarlet poppies,
evoking Monet by the Risborough road;
Family (in lieu of parasolled ladies)
backpack the footpath through a sea of gold.

Caught in an eye blink, a memory captured:
footpathed family in the waist high corn;
flaxen haired child smiles above the wheat ears,
bobbing towards the distant hedged hawthorn.

OCTOBER

Remembered glory of the Monet meadow
takes me back along the Risborough road;
gone the poppy flowers of burning Summer,
brown trees shiver as the wind blows cold.

Did Monet paint his meadow in Autumn? –
dried stubble stalks make a poor canvas;
here Dashwood's orb reflects the sunset,
copper Autumn trees burn across the grass.

Without swirling wheat, willowherb and poppies,
movement and colour live in distant trees;
she is back, lone figure on the footpath,
wending through the stubble in the evening breeze.

Patrick Osada

When shadowed days are done

Don't tell me something I already know:
of stars and Summer evenings' after glow,
how Autumn brings the single rose grown thin
and Winter, lonely footprints in the snow.

Don't talk of falling leaves and failing light,
thin rain and solitary birds in flight;
forget the shadows creeping up the wall
and how dusk disappears, replaced by night.

Sing to me sunshine – glorious dawn above,
sparkling seas, gentle breeze, two cooing doves;
don't listen for the last chime of the clock –
just come to me and only talk of love.

Patrick Osada

'When orange is the sky'
오렌]을 너머

Even during this violent storm
peace can be found in the rain.
In the beat of birds' wings.
The orange sunset.
Bluish dusk hour
holds clear skies
and still
lakes.
Stars
and moon
reflected
in its black depths.
A powerful crescent
monochromatic moon
beyond reach of orange skies
beyond grasp of the storms and rains.

Lillie Postlewhite

Inevitable
불가피한

At least I can watch as the cherry blossom fall,
flutter down in peaceful chaos to the damp ground.
I'm reminded of where the Heron stand tall.

It's already the season of a mother bird's call,
time for new life to form and new selves to be found.
At least I can watch as the cherry blossom fall

if not discover myself. Chicks squawk and babies bawl
and I sit amongst it within my writing, drowned.
I'm reminded of where a Heron stood tall.

Oversees, river to lake. Crossing channels, as if owning all
her eyes land upon. Her head should be crowned.
At least I can watch as the cherry blossom fall

before going back to that place, for the long haul.
Herons fly above me now, is she among their sound?
At least I can watch as the cherry blossom fall,
and be reminded of where that Heron stood tall.

Lillie Postlewhite

A pub in Wales

It was lunchtime.
The sun was shining.
We went inside.

No one said much.
Nowhere to sit,
in this small pub.

I went towards some swing doors, tried to push one open. I had to lean on it, as if a huge weight lay behind it. A blast of talking and chinking of cutlery came through the gap and a whoosh of warm bodies and hot food rushed past my face.

I was looking into darkness, without any walls. Thousands of small lights, and tiers of tables and people lay before me, as if I'd stepped on the stage of a grand opera house with an infinite audience, talking, and waiting for something.

And they were laughing, eating, drinking, shrieking, as they recognised people they knew, walking up and down from one tier to another, revelling in the joy, the love they had for each other on this other side of the swing doors.

I knew I'd never find what they were waiting for. And I thought, perhaps, that this was going on all day, every day. I let the swing door close and as it did, the warmth, the noise, squeezed into an inch gap and the door flopped shut.

We ordered lunch.
No one went through
the swing doors.

I didn't tell my friends.
They would have taken
it all away from me.

Victoria Pugh

The enemy within

He drags the hammered metal doors apart,
creaking open. The smell of trapped time,
the cool embrace of preserved silence,
darkness flowering out of the walls.
He pushes his flame ahead of him,
on, on, down twisted corridors,
in the coils inside his head.
There's roaring, shrieking;
he raises his shield,
draws his sword,
lunges at him,
half-man,
half-beast,
Minotaur.

Minotaur.
Half-beast
half-man,
lunges at him,
draws his sword.
He raises his shield.
There's roaring, shrieking
in the coils inside his head.
On, on down twisted corridors
he pushes his flame ahead of him,
darkness flowering out of the walls.
The cool embrace of preserved silence.
Creaking open the smell of trapped time,
he drags the hammered metal doors apart.

Victoria Pugh

Curlews

'I take my gladness in the sound of the curlew rather than the laughter of men'
— the Seafarer *c.* 1000 AD.

Curlews are now on the red list of endangered species.

Possessors of wide, windy uplands,
flattened grasses, archipelagos
of cloud and reed and peat,
these messengers from otherwhere.

Their bubbling, upward-turning cry starts,
stops, returns – antiphonal farewell.

Kate Pursglove

Stanley's War

Sandham Memorial Chapel

We dug their graves and left them, mules and men.
Left them to wait as they had, times before,
and when Reveille sounds they'll rise again.

We gave them bread and jam, hay, iodine,
and scraped their feet when frostbite made them sore.
We dug their graves and left them, mules and men.

We played Last Post, piled on the earth and then
stood easy, had a fry-up, scrubbed the floor.
And when Reveille sounds they'll rise again.

They'll scramble for their boots and climb out when
Jesus appears to summon up the corps.
We dug their graves and left them, mules and men,
and when Reveille sounds they'll surely rise again.

Kate Pursglove

The Wrong Way Round

I didn't expect this:
a spring morning so cold
it hurts to breathe.

Flurries of snowflakes
spin in sunshine, mingle
with petals of pear blossom.

Easter colder than Christmas,
new leaves edged with frost –
it's the wrong way round.

Each time I see you
you are further away.
I lift your pale hand, don't want

to let go. This is all wrong
like April snow.

Susan Roberts

The Ides of March

The nurse arrives early with a bright smile, shakes
her umbrella, props it in the porch, steps inside.

Don't let him see those tears, she whispers,
as she puts on her apron. I turn away,

take my cold cup of tea to the window,
watch children skipping through puddles to school.

The sky is weeping with me, not in torrents,
just a steady gentle rainfall, and I wonder

will it ever stop? The cherry tree in the street
has burst into blossom, shocking pink against grey.
Somewhere, I suppose, it must be spring.

Susan Roberts

Putting You in the Picture

after 'Infringement', Rebecca Swainston,
oil and printing ink on canvas

The bad creature leaps on the table. It knows this
is not allowed, but the girl is holding out her hand,

wants her palm tickled. A cup is about to tip, crash
to the floor, and neither of them will do anything

to stop it. (Someone else in the room can see it too.)
A pair of shoes crouches beneath the table like mice

who witness but do not understand what manner
of trespass the stool was committing when a hind foot

rested there for a second. The table is on trestles,
at any moment they could buckle and collapse –

which is why someone else is standing at the ready,
a steadying hand. But soon everything will be packed up

and shoved away somewhere like one of those box sets
to be binged on and never quite finished.

Lesley Saunders

The Other Woman

after 'Trying It On', Rebecca Swainston,
oil and printing ink on canvas

I am not myself today, I am trying on
a wardrobe of best frocks so I can feel

what it is like to be beautiful and brave,
to have an alter ego I can wrap myself in

for a second skin, because my day-sleeves
reveal how starved my arms have become

in their grief; because my almost-cleavage
is insufficient to save me; because I am

wide-awake and waiting – here she comes
to hoodwink me, with her asterisks for eyes

and her whispers at my ear, her lips pursing
an apology even as she steals my shoes;

she cranes towards me, my shadow-self,
her stain spreading over the walls of my room.

Lesley Saunders

Wounded Sky

If you spent all your life on a stage then suddenly
you're asked to play yourself but don't know how

because all the past and present is at once contained
bottled up in the coming second you drain it

gulp it down and you just consumed all history
not just the shadow but the whole

does this knowledge have a colour, even a shade
your face appears in other years lighting up

as you run your hooves over this do you hope to find
a pattern like a chessboard of ploughed and fallow fields

of gentle paw-prints of unexpected size
do they have a focus; orange, cinnamon, grey

dark chestnut, a key, do they have a voice you can't
make anyone value you who simply doesn't

will you, will the cold claw inside you, claw to the bone
will the rising sun, will the clock in your head

print odd words in red in the great church Bible
will it sing, will it heal, will you speak

and each new breath is another bottle of all time
in your own voice at the last?

Geoff Sawers

Ton Up No Lights

Was anyone up for a hurley she asked
and no one knew what she meant
but no one said
the reservoir was rising
it had rained for weeks
bats flung on the wind
wolves outpaced by the reservation boundary
begin to exit here, press six for escape
the steering-wheel had a life of its own
all night we heard voices
in her eyes was a sweat of real fear
but no hope of turning back
all ghosts at the wheel, we were god, we were go
and we were the stars ourselves, the bats, the rain
we were in and of the wind and
we were rising

Geoff Sawers

When Christ Came to Glastonbury

When Christ came to Glastonbury did anyone recognise him,
    I wonder,
as we search the town for a place that might sell a Cornetto,
distinguish him in a line-up of doppelgangers,
in his simple clothes, loose curls, bare feet.
Did he cry, slumped at the door of the Methodist church,
lie out the afternoon in a graveyard of primroses?
Or did he twirl in the streets, tie-dyed, bright-eyed,
try aromatherapy for healing like this miracle remedy
    for lethargy,
or spot this strange effigy
of a medieval knight jousting with a plaster of Paris statue
    of his mother
while over on the corner – ten-foot-plus in his stilts –
a modern-day Joseph of Arimathea shares a beer
with a bona fide wizard.
Or perhaps he was too busy stocking up on boxes of fairy dust
at six pounds a throw
to hear the psychic interpret his tarot
on this painted pavement
streaked with a halo
of chalks
to reflect
the rainbow.
I expect so.
Meanwhile, we continue our quest for an ice-cream, slowed,
    now by the joining of
a three-pound polar bear teddy named Crystal,
a red bow tie and
a real-life
angel.

Isobel Shirlaw

Candle

Faith is a candle –
a simple block of wax
moulded
from a relief
that even the hottest flame
may still be held
in the palm
of an
open
hand.

Here –

take my heart.

Show me the way.

Isobel Shirlaw

the something unsaid

the blank space with something, said
sort of
       almost
(maybe it's missing a step
          maybe i'm missing
something, said)
strictly speaking
         i always forget

the something (i think it's left unsaid)
sleeping in speaking,
        the thought that's slipping
(it's likely i'm
         forgetting again)

the weighted way of the something unsaid
i know i could've,
        would've and should've,
but i think some things are better left unsaid

Megan Slater

the night-walk exhibition

four sides in a frame,
the blueness of dusk and
the yellow light, looking
    glance for a second – just a second, and

    i'm picturing the place you sat on
    a Tuesday evening, two winters ago
    a Countdown repeat on in the background
    your cat on your lap and your mum down the phone
    telling you *i got a washer-dryer on the cheap,*
    i'll get you the discount, and –

side-by-side wall divide,
a light a little whiter, now
with spider plants and snake plants
    and a condensation from cooking, i think

    you're making bolognese for four
    herbs and garlic and tinned tomatoes
    enough for five or six, even though
    your son will make a plate-side pile
    of onion slices, scraped or
    pieces of mince he decides he doesn't like

across the street, thirty-eight
a gate broken by wind
and netting showing silhouettes
    making out the shapes of the

    backdrop of lamplight, and you
    (the shadow-person), idle
    at the dining table
    with your shadow-person,
    you'll ask about each other's day

      and say something rude about your manager
      and something ruder about your mother,

and that *we should really invest in*
some new curtains, i keep telling you
to draw them in the evening,
there's a stranger looking in again

Megan Slater

Emily in Paris, too

That we watched the whole three series
in a week. You, me, all the fashion,
and bucket hats and *rangard* and décolletage.

So much cliché – Tuileries picnics, the French men
with their charm and shirts unbuttoned just so,
their champagne. And all the time I ask you –

Do you remember? Do you remember?
The heatwave at the end of May
before Notre Dame and the world were burning.

Your brother on Rue Jacob, folding white paper boats
into the fountain at Jardin Luxembourg; we ate breakfast
at Le Sorbon, pétanque players from the night before

and it felt like waking. My mother holding,
your hand at Boulevard St. Germain,
summer's lilac light, dinner in Saint Sulpice.

You told me you thought the menu said lion,
and that scared you. And how the years dissolve
like sugar on the squares of your gaufre.

From here, we watch it all unfold –
heartbreak and lavender and dog shit,
impossible elegance and I say –

Let's go back, darling, let's go back.

Antonia Taylor

Spring lunchtimes,
I knew you'd be waiting

by the gate of our old school,
the wrought iron one the Brits left.
Holding the hot chicken sandwich

with coleslaw nobody made like you.
Always too much mayo and your full weight
against the turquoise Hillman we all hated.

So in your body that now you're not,
do the cypress trees still breathe
their clay? You always found people.

Like when you met a childhood friend
with a whole war and an island
split in on itself and between you.

I was half in love with his son –
I heard he moved to LA now.
That I didn't think what a thing:

to drive half-way across a small city
white with grief, all of you wrapped
in grease paper – sesame seed bread,

burgers for the boys, the orange carton
that gave me headaches. Turns out
I'm allergic and I never told you.

That you made those lunches
with your hands and your time
and your sorry. Before your blood

turned, the calls, that last trip home.
Could you find me now?
I'll share my lunch with you.

Take a bite, take half,
take the whole thing.
I saved it all this time.

Antonia Taylor

Absolutely Everything

After Derek Mahon, 'Everything is Going to be All Right'

Everything is going to be alright: electrons
will continue to be in two places at once,
Alvinella Pompejana will thrive in its trillions,
beetles will dominate the taxonomic tables;
rats, mice, voles and squirrels will be
everywhere, human beings will continue
to prosper, at least for a time, as species
come and go, come and go. The earth will
keep capering round one of billions of stars,
solar systems will whiz and galaxies progress
in a stately manner at near the speed of light.
Yes, everything's going to be alright, because
although the universe will expand and expand
then contract and collapse into nothingness,
God will wake with a start from His slumber,
reach over and press the Start button again.

Robin Thomas

Gedicht gefunden

Your kitchen is much too small
I don't like the refrigerator
Oh no the microwave is really dirty
The cooker is new and not yet dirty

I cook the potato
The vegetables are in the sandwich
Tim and Maria, do you want to eat sausage?
Don't eat so much schnitzel Lisa

Why is there a cucumber in the living room?
Why does your grandmother have so many oranges?
Grandma and Grandpa, are you Germans?
Why do you have two hundred potatoes in the suitcase?

Robin Thomas

All the above sentences are contained in the German course
of a well-known educational technology company.

The Colour of Dark

I walk until the shade runs out,
then turn, pause, retrace my steps
under trees, through gaps between
fat bushes, up against high fences.

Sun is blinding – I mean no metaphor,
sunlight destroys our sight, the fair-
skinned, blue, hazel, green-eyed people,
year by year its rays dim our foveae.

Deep shade delights me: it is every
colour, from late evening's purple
to the grey flannel of mysterious dusk.
It's taken a whole life to see true dark,

to know it's nothing to be scared of. When
there is no light, no torch, candle, lantern,
bulb or fire, there's no more wickedness
than in the light; evil doesn't care.

Susan Utting

Wired for Sound

Soft-spoken women, coverers of lips,
ventriloquising girls who speak through smiles,
young mumblers, heavy-bearded men:
I love the sounds your mouths make, each
to each across a wide space. I close my eyes
and listen to the tilt and slant of syllables,
the flavour of each word, your agile tongue-tricks,
breaths and lisps, your accenting and chattering.

The dull and flat of everyday, the glitter
of kind platitudes, the easy-speak of strangers,
the brickie's wit, the world's banter and chunter,
I hear it all: my ears are wired, sharpened,
switched on to all the jangle and racket, filled
with the thrill of noise, the heady joy of hearing.

Susan Utting

Llanrhaeadr

He kept his arm round me all the way –
the boy I'd only just met and would never see again.

All along the narrow valley I kept chattering
to ward off further advances, and he made none,

just said goodnight when we reached the caravan,
strode off into the night. Then I looked up

to see a symphony of stars, so bright –
no smokescreen or streetlights between us.

They seemed in a slow slow waltz around unlimited space
and I was a speck on Earth's forehead.

Jean Watkins

Tulips

For almost a week they'd stood demurely,
turbans from the ancient east. Given fresh water

they flopped, hung over the side, but later
I was shocked to see a surreal artwork, threatening.

The heads had risen, stems straining to an S
like snakes – the serpents in Medusa's crown.

Their crimson petals spread wider and wider
exposing the yellow centre and black stamens –

in that closed room they seemed to be craving,
longing for a bee, for sex, a consummation.

Jean Watkins

Cor Cordium (Heart of Hearts)

From the inscription on Shelley's headstone

Kindling pricks the small of my back
presses into cold, quick-limed flesh.
If I could I would stretch and scratch.
Friends, you've drenched me in frankincense
wine and salt, wrapped me in a cotton shift.
Once young and handsome, now
– *pale even to the lips…* I've become
the food of fish, limbs pulled and picked.
If I could look in the glass I would see
an eyeless face, pearly as the belly of squid.
My wasted body, storm-battered and lost,
washed up on Viareggio beach;
you knew me by my jacket, and within
the breast pocket, a borrowed volume
of Keats' Lamia, which I now return
in poor condition, pages bleached, as if:
Upon a time, before the faery broods…
suffused my heart via cloth and skin.

If I could, I would walk right now with you
Byron, Hunt, Trelawny, along this wild shore
at the mouth of the Serchio, gathering
driftwood, talking of romance and ideas
– we young men, with hope and desire –
amid soft curling waves, the light brush of air.
Alas! I have nor hope nor health,
Nor peace within nor calm around…

Now, without my help you hold up high
the lighted torch, then touch it to the hungry wood.
If I could, I would breathe as I burn...
Scatter, as from an unextinguished hearth
Ashes and sparks, my words among mankind!
And when the heat is down, the grey ash
cooling, you begin to rake and scoop,
wanting for something left behind –
something to signify the fiery poet's art
Thirsting to eclipse their burning
In a sea of death and mourning...
there you find my smouldering heart.

Ann Westgarth

How to hang Ruth Ellis

Like all the others it begins with the opening
of the hangman's box, wherein lie tools of death
and the coiled noose like a sleeping serpent
waiting to be awakened. Sometimes called
the 'Bridport Dagger', this efficient rope
is crafted from a hybrid of hemp and flax,
by women whose roughened hands
are a far cry from Ruth Ellis' soft sexualised
skin. Her confession to her lover's murder,
uncompromising, 'it was obvious
when I shot him, I intended to kill him'.

She is led now by Albert Pierrepoint, executioner,
to the mark on the floor, above which the cord
is slung. A white hood is placed over her blonde
coiffured hair, scarlet lips, and pale chin. Albert
allows his hand to linger, as he positions the ring,
through which the rope passes, under the left
side of her jaw. There, in a few seconds' time
when the door opens and the prisoner drops,
her head will be forced back, spine snapped.

In the stillness before the act, she exhales
a long deep breath as if in ecstasy. A shaft
of light slices the high cell wall, dry dust rises.
A lacewing flutters long wings against the pane.
Albert Pierrepoint pushes the heavy lever,
the trapdoor thuds open; Ruth Ellis falls.

Ann Westgarth

The Gift of Darkness

Why would anyone rage
against the dying of the light?
Was it your parents who taught you
to be afraid, leaving you alone
at night with just the rectangular glow
around the door's edge?

And even now, the adult in you
who drags everything said and done
behind you is grateful for the pinpricked
star-frosted dome of a night sky,
and the flares falling from the street lamps,
house windows, shop-fronts.

You still have to learn, the absence
of light is not heavy but fine
as a cobweb, as natural as death:
that deep unending breath –

Jules Whiting

Rather than video games

comes the thought of a blade of grass
stretched between finger and thumb,
pulled tight as lips blast its tension,
to a wild shriek.

Or the way white floaties tickle your nose
when you dandelion blow the time to fourteen o'clock.
Or finger comb meadow-foxtail, sedge, cocksfoot,
looking for that magical four-leaf clover.

I wish I could take you to our back doorstep,
the World Service wallpapering each Sunday,
a roast spitting its juice. Us shelling peas,
our mouths filled with greenness.

Jules Whiting

Contributors

Liam Anslow-Sucevic was born and raised in Milton Keynes. He is currently a Creative Writing PhD student at the University of Reading; his research concerns the intersections between the archive, the elegy, and visuality.

Kate Behrens' fourth collection, *Transitional Spaces* was published by Two Rivers Press in April 2022. Other poems have appeared in journals and anthologies including *Mslexia*, *The High Window* and *Poetry Salzburg Review*. Kate has been attending South Street's Poets Café for many years and has appeared there as their guest poet. Through Two Rivers Press she has joined Reading poets for readings in Reading, London and Oxford.

Denise Bundred was a consultant paediatric cardiologist and began writing poetry in retirement. She is a Fellow of the Royal College of Physicians and holds an MA in Writing. Denise won the Hippocrates Prize for Poetry and Medicine in 2016, coming second in 2019. Her poems have appeared in magazines including *Magma* and *Prole*; and various anthologies including the *Hippocrates Prize Anthologies* and *These are the Hands: NHS Poetry*. Denise's pamphlet, *Litany of a Cardiologist*, was published by Against the Grain Press in 2020.

J. A. Clothier is a writer and reporter born and raised in Reading. He still remembers when Marilyn Monroe used to stand on Oxford Road and hears 'hot doughnuts, nice and fresh' every time he's on Broad Street. His love of poetry was ignited while studying in Swansea, but since returning he has thoroughly enjoyed taking part in Reading's own vibrant poetry scene. In his work, he combines modern experiences and phenomena with traditional rhyme, metre, and structure, often with a humorous angle.

Maisie Crittenden is currently studying for her Masters in Creative Writing at the University of Reading. She serves as the Captain of the University's women's rugby team and coaches their American Football team, fostering a strong cultural connection with many aspects of the town. Maisie perceives Reading through both a creative lens and a sense of team loyalty and legacy. Reading has been instrumental in her development as a poet as well as an individual.

Marcin Czyż is originally from East Poland and Central Europe and has lived in Reading since 2017. He is an independent warehouseman and casual stage technician. He likes to contemplate his own identity: Genthe Rhuteni, Natione Britani. He loves cooking and painting: Borsch UK & Ukrainian Jack. Marcin helps raising Fryderyk.

Fiona Dignan grew up in Wokingham and went to secondary school in Reading, moving back to Wokingham seven years ago. She started writing during lockdown to cope with the chaos of homeschooling four young children. Since then, her poetry has been published in *Mslexia*, *Popshot* and *Streetcake* magazines. Fiona has won the London Society Poetry Prize, the Plaza Prize for Sudden Fiction and the Anansi Winter Poetry Prize.

Jo Farrant is an emerging poet currently studying Art and Creative Writing at the University of Reading. Their work can be found in *The Canvas Magazine* and *Kite Strings* poetry magazine published by Words Space Poems & The Guitar Social Ltd. Feeling deeply connected to Reading since it became their new home whilst studying at University, Jo often likes to write and create on walks through the town's many green spaces.

John Froy has lived in Reading since 1986. He managed a decorating business in the town and ran local publisher Two Rivers Press in its early days. A prize-winning poet, his work has appeared in anthologies and journals; he has three collections with Two Rivers: *Eggshell* (2007), *Sandpaper & Seahorses* (2018) and *The Blue Armchair* (2024).

Anastasia Gale is 18 years old and was born in Reading at the Royal Berkshire Hospital to a long maternal line of Wokingham residents. Living in Lower Earley until the age of seven, she moved to Swindon for ten years and now lives in Woodley. Currently a first-year student at the University of Reading, Anastasia is studying for a Joint BA in English Literature and Film.

Martin Haslam has lived in the Reading area for forty-five years. He worked as a family doctor in Wokingham for thirty years. He has been a member of an established circle of Reading poets for many years and has been a regular contributor at Reading's Poets' Café. He has had poems short-listed for the Troubadour International Poetry Prize on two occasions.

Kitty Hawkins moved from Norfolk to study undergraduate English Literature and Creative Writing at the University of Reading. She volunteered as Editor of *The Canvas*, the university's arts anthology, and produced the magazine's first issue. Kitty received the Margaret Seymour and Percy Sharman Prize, and the Rosalind Laker Award for her dissertation and final poetry collection, *Acoustics*. Kitty continued to live in Reading while studying for her MA in Creative Writing at Royal Holloway, graduating in 2022. She won the 'Magdalena Young Poet' award in 2022.

Megan Hay first came to Reading in 2020 to study an English literature and creative writing degree at the University of Reading. Previous to this she had never written any poetry, but once she began writing for her degree, writing poetry became a habit that she could not stop. Her time spent in Reading for those three years kickstarted her love for writing, and for that very reason, she now associates Reading with being closer to her own creativity.

Frances Hudson is currently an undergraduate student at the University of Reading studying English literature and Creative Writing. Poetry has always been a deep love of hers, exercised through her poetry Instagram @square_girl_ and via her position as co-editor of *The Canvas*, a student-led literary and arts magazine. In 2019, she collaboratively organised a summer arts festival with the Chelmsford Creatives youth group and Chelmsford Museum, with whom she also helped to create the Boredom-19 zine, a zine focusing on the experiences of young people during the Covid-19 pandemic.

Karen Izod works an academic and consultant to organisations. Her writing focuses on place and landscape, on thin places, city spaces, people, politics, and memories that trace across generations. Her writing is published by, amongst others: *Agenda*, *Interpreter's House*, *New Welsh Review*, *Corrupted Poetry*, and she has been short-listed in The Bridport Prize's poetry and flash fiction competitions (2021/22). She has written for the British Council of Psychoanalyis, for the Tavistock Institute and Tavistock and Portman NHS Trust. She was winner of *Coast to Coast to Coast*'s single poet pamphlet competition in 2021. Karen participates in her local poetry communities in Guildford, Woking, Reading and the south-east.

Andrew Jamison was born in Co. Down, Northern Ireland in 1986. Having studied for his BA in London, and the MLitt in Creative Writing at St Andrews, he's published two collections of poetry with Gallery Press (*Happy Hour* in 2012, and *Stay* in 2017). His third is forthcoming in later this year. He lives in Oxfordshire with his family, and teaches English at Abingdon School. Alongside this, he is a part-time PhD candidate at the University of Reading; his thesis is concerned with surveillance in contemporary poetry from the North of Ireland. His poetry has been published widely in the UK and further afield.

Charlotte Johnson came to Reading in 1995, considering it a temporary move. Thirty years later she is still a Reading resident. She has read her work on BBC Berkshire, been published in *The Canvas* and *Popshot Magazine*. She was selected to represent the South East in the Apples and Snakes Future Voices programme and created a poetic film about Reading Festival. Charlotte is a member of Reading Stanza.

Zannah Kearns is a copywriter in the charity sector. Her poems have appeared in journals such as *Poetry Birmingham Literary Journal*, *The Dark Horse*, *Finished Creatures*, *Under the Radar*, *South* and online with *Ink, Sweat & Tears* and *Atrium*. She was an iamb poet in December 2022, and has just finished her first play, commissioned by the University of Reading's Law Department about the Post Office Horizon scandal.

Gill Learner has lived in Reading since 1966. Her poems have been published in print magazines including *Acumen*, *Agenda*, *14*, *The French Literary Review*, *The Interpreter's House*, *North*, *Orbis*, *Poetry Bulletin*, *Mslexia* and *South*; and online in *The High Window* and *Canvas*; also in a number of anthologies e.g. from The Emma Press, Grey Hen Press, HappenStance Press, Second Light Publications and Two Rivers Press, and won prizes including the Poetry Society's Hamish Canham Award and the Buxton Prize (twice). Her three collections, *The Agister's Experiment* (2011), *Chill Factor* (2016) and *Change* (2021) are all from Two Rivers Press.

Katherine Meehan lives in Reading. Her work has appeared at *Magma*, *The Kenyon Review*, *Anthropocene*, and other journals. Her first collection, *Dame Julie Andrews' Botched Vocal Cord Surgery*, was published by Two Rivers Press in 2023. She is a co-organiser of Reading's Poets' Cafe.

Kate Noakes' eighth poetry collection is *Goldhawk Road* (Two Rivers Press, 2023). She has degrees in Geography, and English Literature from Reading University and an MPhil in Creative Writing from the University of South Wales. She has recently completed a PhD at the University of Reading. She lives in London and when not writing is a printmaker. Further details on Kate and her work can be found at www.boomslangpoetry.blogspot.com

Louise Ordish is a poet who's lived in Reading and the surrounding area for twenty years and whose poetry hub and home is *Reading Stanza*. Her work has been published in magazines including *Envoi* and *Mslexia* and shortlisted in publishing competitions run by *The Poetry Business* and Nine Arches Press. 2022 saw her returning to writing after a break in which she retrained as a therapist.

Patrick Osada's work has been broadcast on national and local radio and widely published in magazines, anthologies and on the internet. His first collection, *Close to the Edge*, was published in 1996 and since then he has published a further six books – his most recent, *From The Family Album*, was launched in October 2020. Patrick recently retired after ten years on *SOUTH* Poetry Magazine's Management Team and as the Magazine's Reviews Editor.

Lillie Postlewhite has lived in Reading for the past four years. Though her time living in the town draws to a close, these poems serve as a commemoration of her experiences at Reading. The poems have two titles, one in English and one in Korean. Korea has become Lillie's third home after studying abroad there through the University of Reading.

Victoria Pugh's first collection of poetry, *Mrs Marvellous*, was published by Two Rivers Press in 2008. A poem from this collection was highly commended and published in The Forward Book of Poetry, 2009. She has been successful in competitions and has had her work published in various poetry magazines.

Kate Pursglove has lived in Reading for nearly fifty years, teaching in the town as well as facilitating the 'Continuing to find the words' poetry group. Kate's work has been published in Reading University's Creative Arts Anthology and she regularly reads at Poets' Café.

Susan Roberts came to live in Reading many years ago, as a nineteen-year-old newlywed. Her first home in the town was a flat in Baker Street, and she worked in a day nursery, an advertising agency and latterly for a charity. Quickly coming to know and love the town, Susan brought up three children in Reading. Susan has participated in a number of writing workshops and been a Poets' Café regular for many years.

Lesley Saunders has had several collections of poetry and poems in translation published by Two Rivers Press, beginning in 1998 with *Christina the Astonishing*, which was co-authored with Jane Draycott and recently re-issued. During the first year of the Covid pandemic, Lesley discovered the work of Rebecca Swainston, an internationally-renowned artist who lives in Tilehurst, and the pair worked together to create a book of poems and images in response to those times; it was published as *Days of Wonder* by Hippocrates Press in 2021.

Geoff Sawers' poetry publications include *Scissors Cut Rock* (Flarestack, 2005) and *A Thames Bestiary* (with Peter Hay; Two Rivers Press 2008). He also wrote 'Silver In My Mines: Peter Hay's work for Two Rivers Press 1994–2003' (University at Buffalo, New York, 2021).

Isobel Shirlaw is a writer based in Reading. In 2019 she won the Fresher Poetry Prize and was highly commended in the Poetry Space competition. Her poetry has appeared in wildfire words online magazine. She has reviewed books for *The i*, *TLS*, *Daily Telegraph* and Bangladeshi broadsheets, *New Age* and *Daily Star*. Her debut novel is scheduled for publication in 2024 and she is represented by Jon Wood of RCW literary agency.

Megan Slater is a third-year student currently studying Art and Creative Writing (BA) at the University of Reading. Originally from an estate in Milton Keynes, much of her poetry stems from experiences of social class, whilst also turning to the experience of the everyday – although, always based in memory.

Antonia Taylor is a British Cypriot writer, communications expert, and poet. Her work has appeared in *Propel*, *Ambit*, *Harana*, *South*, *New Contexts*, *Blood Moon Poetry*, *Marble Magazine*, *Dear Reader* and *Indelible Literary Journal*. She lives in Reading with her family.

Robin Thomas is a long-term resident of Reading. He has had poems published in *Agenda*, *Envoi*, *Orbis*, *Brittle Star*, *Poetry Salzburg*, *Poetry Scotland*, *Pennine Platform*, T*he High Window*, *South*, *Stand*, *Rialto*, *The Interpreters House*, *Acumen*, *Tears in the Fence* and *North*. His pamphlet *A Fury of Yellow*, was published by Eyewear in 2016. His collections *Momentary Turmoil*, *A Distant Hum* and *Reminded of Something* were published by Cinnamon in 2018, 2021 and 2023 respectively. His pamphlet *Cafferty's Truck* was published by Dempsey and Windle in 2021 and his *The Weather on the Moon* by Two Rivers Press in 2022.

Susan Utting graduated in English from Reading University, prior to which she had worked briefly in The Careers Advisory Service, and then for many years in the Psychology Department. She subsequently taught poetry and creative writing at Reading and Oxford Universities for more than 17 years. Her New & Selected Poems, *Half the Human Race*, was published in 2017, followed by her fifth full collection *The Colour of Rain* in 2024. Susan was the original host of Reading's Poets' Café in the 1990s.
www.susanutting.com

Jean Watkins has lived near Reading for over fifty years. She studied at the University, including Creative Writing, and attended Poets' Café regularly. Her poems have been widely published in magazines and anthologies, and she has two collections, *Scrimshaw* and *Precarious Lives* published by Two Rivers Press.

Ann Westgarth has lived and worked in Reading for many years, first as a youth worker and then in community engagement for the local authority and the university. Ann qualified as an English teacher, has an MA in Creative Writing from the University of Chichester, and has run workshops in writing and poetry for young people and adults. As the co-ordinator of a community-led oral history project, Ann collected the stories of people who came to Reading from all over the world. These oral testimonies are archived in Reading Museum, and are published in the book *Routes to Reading*.

Jules Whiting has a MA in creative writing from Bath Spa University. Shortlisted for Gloucester Prize 2020, commended in the Poetry Society Members Competition 2020, shortlisted, Buzzwords 2020. Her poems have appeared in *Acumen*, *Orbis*, *South*, *Envoi*, *The Interpreters House*, *High Window*, *Haibun Journal* and anthologised widely. A micro-pamphlet, *What colour is my brain?* by Hedgehog Press in collaboration with Vic Pickup, and her debut collection *Folding Time* were published in 2022.

Two Rivers Press has been publishing in and about Reading
since 1994. Founded by the artist Peter Hay (1951–2003),
the press continues to delight readers, local and further afield,
with its varied list of individually designed,
thought-provoking books.

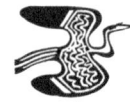